Mifflin
Harcourt

Writing

Grade 1

Copyright © 2014 by Houghton Mifflin Harcourt Publishing Company

All rights reserved. No part of this work may be reproduced or transmitted in any form or by any means, electronic or mechanical, including photocopying or recording, or by any information storage or retrieval system, without the prior written permission of the copyright owner unless such copying is expressly permitted by federal copyright law.

Permission is hereby granted to individuals to photocopy entire pages from this publication in classroom quantities for instructional use and not for resale. Requests for information on other matters regarding duplication of this work should be addressed to Houghton Mifflin Harcourt Publishing Company, Attn: Contracts, Copyrights, and Licensing, 9400 Southpark Center Loop, Orlando, Florida 32819-8647.

Printed in the U.S.A.

ISBN   978-0-5442-6833-3

    5 6 7 8 9 10   0982   22 21 20 19 18 17 16

4500580314   B C D E F G

If you have received these materials as examination copies free of charge, Houghton Mifflin Harcourt Publishing Company retains title to the materials and they may not be resold. Resale of examination copies is strictly prohibited.

Possession of this publication in print format does not entitle users to convert this publication, or any portion of it, into electronic format.

Core Skills Writing

GRADE 1

Table of Contents

© Houghton Mifflin Harcourt Publishing Company

© Houghton Mifflin Harcourt Publishing Company

Table of Contents
Core Skills Writing, Grade 1

Introduction

Writing is one of the core skills necessary for success in school and in life. The better writer a person is, the better that person can communicate with others. Good writing is a skill acquired through guidance, practice, and self-evaluation. This book provides guidance for success in different writing formats. This book also provides many opportunities for writing practice.

Clear writing and clear speaking are products of clear thinking. Clear thinking is a product of good organization of ideas. Good organization is a product of careful planning. One good way to plan is through graphic organizers.

- In this book, different kinds of graphic organizers are provided for children to plan their writing.

- These organizers appeal to the multiple intelligences. They provide children with a visual and tactile approach in their writing.

- Some graphic organizers guide children through specific steps in the writing process. The organizers help them focus on the elements of good writing.

- Other organizers help children organize their writing so as to ensure a successful writing experience.

Organization

This book is divided into nine units. Each unit builds upon earlier units. Using this scaffolded approach, writing becomes like construction.

- **Unit 1: Laying the Foundation** addresses the basic process of writing.

- **Unit 2: Building Sentences** emphasizes the act of writing. Writers learn sentence structure and the different kinds of sentences.

- **Units 3–8** provide guidance and practice writing in different formats such as personal stories, descriptions, friendly letters, and how-to paragraphs. Lessons focus on the basic skills needed to develop well-written paragraphs, including parts of speech and writing traits. Writers also follow the writing process to craft a work using each form. Space to write is included to help students organize and follow the writing process more easily.

- **Unit 9: Resources** offers writers basic materials in one place for easy reference. They will find charts detailing the writing process, a proofreading checklist, proofreading marks, and language tips.

Write Away

For too many children, writing is a struggle or a pain. They may not realize the benefits of being a good writer, or they may not care. This book tries to reach out to all writers with an approach that allows children to "see" their writing in a new light. Writing does not have to be a chore. It can be fun. Children just have to be reminded that good writing can be their golden ticket to success in school and life.

© Houghton Mifflin Harcourt Publishing Company

Features

Bullets highlight important points of the skill.

Examples model the skill.

A writing activity checks children's understanding.

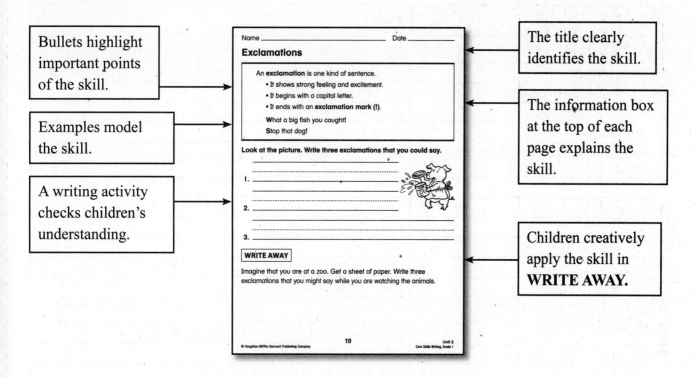

Name _____ Date _____

Exclamations

An **exclamation** is one kind of sentence.
- It shows strong feeling and excitement.
- It begins with a capital letter.
- It ends with an **exclamation mark (!)**.

What a big fish you caught!
Stop that dog!

Look at the picture. Write three exclamations that you could say.

1. _____

2. _____

3. _____

WRITE AWAY

Imagine that you are at a zoo. Get a sheet of paper. Write three exclamations that you might say while you are watching the animals.

19

© Houghton Mifflin Harcourt Publishing Company   Unit 2   Core Skills Writing, Grade 1

The title clearly identifies the skill.

The information box at the top of each page explains the skill.

Children creatively apply the skill in **WRITE AWAY.**

All inclusive, multiple pages guide children through the writing process.

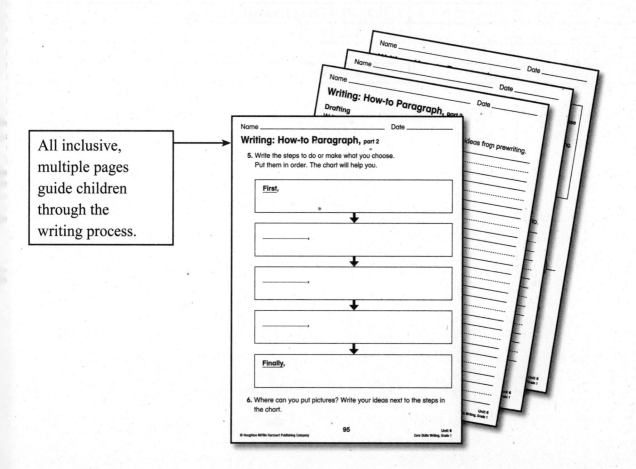

Name _____ Date _____

Writing: How-to Paragraph, part 2

5. Write the steps to do or make what you choose. Put them in order. The chart will help you.

First,

_____

_____

_____

Finally,

6. Where can you put pictures? Write your ideas next to the steps in the chart.

95

© Houghton Mifflin Harcourt Publishing Company   Unit 6   Core Skills Writing, Grade 1

© Houghton Mifflin Harcourt Publishing Company

Features

Core Skills Writing, Grade 1

Skills Correlation

Skill	Page
Types of Writing	
Opinion Paragraph	113, 114, 117, 118, 119, 120, 121
Informative/Explanatory Paragraph	100, 107, 108, 109, 110, 111, 112
Personal Narrative Paragraph	29, 30, 34, 35, 36, 37, 38, 39, 40, 41, 42, 43, 44, 45
How-to Paragraph	83, 84, 85, 90, 93, 94, 95, 96, 97, 98, 99
Recall information from Experience/Gather Information to Answer a Question	29, 34, 35, 37, 38, 40, 41, 42, 43, 44, 45, 103, 105, 107, 108, 109, 110, 111, 112
Journal	3, 122
Story	3
Poster	3
List	3
Description	62, 77, 78, 79, 80, 81, 82
Friendly Letter	3, 46, 53, 54, 55, 57, 58, 59, 60, 61
Writing Process	
Prewriting	5, 6, 24, 40, 41, 57, 77, 78, 94, 95, 107, 108, 117, 123
Drafting	7, 25, 42, 58, 79, 96, 109, 118, 123
Revising	8, 26, 43, 80, 93, 97, 110, 119, 123
Peer Editing	7, 8, 26, 43, 80, 93, 97, 110, 119
Proofreading	9, 10, 23, 27, 44, 60, 81, 98, 111, 120, 123
Focusing on a Topic	12, 102, 107, 108, 110, 114
Adding Details	8, 26, 37, 40, 43, 62, 72, 74, 75, 77, 78, 100, 104
Publishing/Publishing Using a Computer	11, 27, 44, 60, 81, 98, 111, 120

© Houghton Mifflin Harcourt Publishing Company

Skills Correlation, continued

Skill	Page
Vocabulary	
Words with Like Meanings	87
Words with Opposite Meanings	88
Words That Sound Alike	89
Time-Order Words	85
Direction Words	86
Sentences	
Recognizing Sentences and Sentence Types	13, 14, 15, 16, 17, 18, 19, 126
Subject and Predicates	14, 15
Expanding Sentences	20, 68, 69, 72
Run-on Sentences	21
Paragraph Structure	75
Grammar and Usage	
Nouns	14, 30, 31, 32, 33, 52, 126
Verbs	15, 47, 48, 49, 50, 51
Pronouns	29, 56
Adjectives	20, 63, 64, 65, 66, 67, 115
Capitalization and Punctuation	
Capitalization: First Word in Sentence	17, 18, 19, 126
Capitalization: Proper Nouns	31, 52, 126
End Punctuation	17, 18, 19, 126
Commas	53, 70
Book Titles	105

© Houghton Mifflin Harcourt Publishing Company

Writing Rubric

Score of 4

The child:

- clearly follows the writing process,
- demonstrates an understanding of the purpose for writing,
- expresses creativity,
- presents the main idea and supports it with relevant detail,
- presents content in a logical order and sequence,
- uses variety in sentence type and length,
- adjusts writing style to fit the audience,
- uses language appropriate to the writing task, such as language rich in sensory details,
- uses vocabulary to suit purpose and audience, and
- has few or no errors in the standard rules of English grammar, punctuation, capitalization, and spelling.

Score of 3

The child:

- generally follows the criteria described above, and
- has some errors in the standard rules of English grammar, punctuation, capitalization, and spelling, but not enough to impair a reader's comprehension.

Score of 2

The child:

- marginally follows the criteria described above, and
- has several errors in the standard rules of English grammar, punctuation, capitalization, and spelling, which may impair a reader's comprehension.

Score of 1

The child:

- fails to follow the criteria described above, and
- has many errors in the standard rules of English grammar, punctuation, capitalization, and spelling that impair a reader's comprehension.

© Houghton Mifflin Harcourt Publishing Company

Writing and Talking

You use words when you talk. You use words when you write, too. Writing is like talking.

Look at the picture. Tell someone about it.

WRITE AWAY

What did you say about the picture? Write the words.

_____

- -

_____

- -

_____

- -

_____

- -

_____

1

© Houghton Mifflin Harcourt Publishing Company

A Journal Page

You can write in a **journal**. You can tell about your day.
- Write the date.
- Tell what you do and think.
- Draw a picture if you want.

Write a journal page. Tell what you did today. Draw a picture to go with the words.

_____

- -

Date _____

_____

- -

_____

- -

_____

WRITE AWAY

Start a journal. Make copies of the journal paper on page 122. Staple the pages together.

© Houghton Mifflin Harcourt Publishing Company

Kinds of Writing

There are many kinds of writing. A **journal** is one kind of writing. A **letter** is another kind of writing. You can write a letter to a friend or to your family.

Read the words. Then write a word to name each kind of writing.

story	letter	poster

1.

_____
- - - - - - - - - - - - - - - - -
_____

2.

_____
- - - - - - - - - - - - - - - - -
_____

3. BEARS, BEARS, BEARS

_____
- - - - - - - - - - - - - - - - -
_____

WRITE AWAY

A **list** is another kind of writing. Make a list of your favorite animals.

_____
- -
_____
- -
_____
- -
_____

3

© Houghton Mifflin Harcourt Publishing Company

A Reason to Write

Writers write for a reason.

    A. They tell how they feel.

    B. They want someone to laugh, cry, or get angry.

    C. They teach something.

Look at each picture. Read each reason to write in the box above.
What is the reason for writing? Write the letter under each picture.

1.

2.

3.

_____   _____   _____

-----------------   -----------------   -----------------

_____   _____   _____

WRITE AWAY

What would you like to say about a frog? Write your ideas below.
Write the letter to tell your reason for writing.

_____

_____

_____

© Houghton Mifflin Harcourt Publishing Company

Prewriting: Choosing an Idea

There are steps to take when you write. The steps are called the **writing process**. The steps will help you write.

Prewriting is the first step. You will choose an idea to write about.
- Make a list of ideas.
- Choose one idea.

Read the list. It tells about the first time you may have done something. Write two more ideas.

1. Losing my first tooth

2. Camping for the first time

3. Meeting a new friend

4. Riding a roller coaster for the first time

5. _____

6. _____

WRITE AWAY

Which idea would you like to write about? Write the idea below.

_____

_____

_____

© Houghton Mifflin Harcourt Publishing Company

Prewriting: Making a Web

Prewriting is the first step. You choose an idea to write about.
Then you write words about the idea.

- Make a web.
- Write the idea in the center.
- Write words about the idea around it.

This web will tell about chores. What chores do you do? Write two more chores.

Get a sheet of paper. Tell about a chore that you do not like to do.

© Houghton Mifflin Harcourt Publishing Company

Drafting

Drafting is the second step. You write about your ideas.

Read the story. Write words to complete it.

_____

- -

I go up and down the sidewalk on my _____

_____

- -

I see _____

_____

- -

Sometimes _____ comes with me.

_____

- -

We _____

_____

- -

_____

WRITE AWAY

Ask a family member to read your story. Have
the person look for mistakes. Get a sheet of
paper. Write the story without mistakes.

© Houghton Mifflin Harcourt Publishing Company

Revising

> **Revising** is the third step. You read your draft and make it better. You can share your writing with a partner. Listen to his or her comments. You can add **details.** Adding details makes your writing stronger.

Color the picture. Write words to tell about the clown.

I saw a clown with

_____

- -

_____ hair.

_____

- -

His nose was _____

_____

- -

His hat was _____

WRITE AWAY

Write more details about the clown.

_____

- -

_____

- -

_____

© Houghton Mifflin Harcourt Publishing Company

Proofreading

Proofreading is the fourth step. You will read your writing three times. You will look for one kind of mistake each time.

- Look for words that should begin with a capital letter.
- Look for end marks.
- Look for spelling mistakes.

Read the writing. Circle the mistakes.
(Hint: There are three mistakes.)

It was my birthday? We went to the zo.

it was fun.

WRITE AWAY

Look at the writing above. Write it without mistakes.

_____
- -
_____
- -
_____
- -
_____

© Houghton Mifflin Harcourt Publishing Company

Proofreading Marks

When you edit, you use **proofreading marks.** These special marks tell you what kind of mistakes you see. They show you where the mistakes are.

I planted (seds). I put water on them⊙
They will ∧tall. Someday i̱ will have

F̶lowers.

≡	Use a capital letter.
/	Use a lowercase letter.
⊙	Add a period.
∧	Add something.
⚦	Take out something.
⋏	Change something.
◯	Check the spelling.

Edit the writing. Use proofreading marks.

My frend ted called me He asked me to go to the

Park. I said yes. It would be fun to go the park.

WRITE AWAY

Get a sheet of paper. Write the words above
without mistakes.

© Houghton Mifflin Harcourt Publishing Company

Name _____ Date _____

Publishing on a Computer

Publishing is the last step in the writing process. Use a **computer** to share your writing with others. Always ask an adult before you use a computer. Always **save** your work on a computer. Ask an adult or a friend to show you how.

There are many ways to use a computer to publish your work. Here are some tips.

- Make a **document** to read aloud.

- Make a **slide show** to share.

- Add your writing to a class **blog.**
  The word <u>blog</u> comes from the words <u>web</u> and <u>log</u>.

- Put your writing on a school **podcast.**

- Share your writing on a class **wiki.** The word <u>wiki</u> is a Hawaiian word for <u>quick</u>.

Look at the publishing tips above. Which one do you like best? Write your opinion.

_____

- -

_____

Why do you like it best? Write reasons.

_____

- -

_____

© Houghton Mifflin Harcourt Publishing Company

What to Write

Sometimes you will have to pick a **topic** to write about. The topic is what the writing is mostly about. Choose a topic that you like. Then you will have lots to write about.

Read the topics. Which one would you like to write about? Circle it.

playing soccer   riding a bike

swimming   sledding in the snow

Answer the questions.

1. Why do you like this topic?

_____

- -

_____

- -

_____

2. What is one detail that you will tell?

_____

- -

_____

WRITE AWAY

Get a sheet of paper. Write about the topic you picked.

© Houghton Mifflin Harcourt Publishing Company Core Skills Writing, Grade 1

What Is a Sentence?

A **sentence** is a group of words. It tells a complete thought.

Sentence	**Not a sentence**
The dog sleeps.	The dog.
Boys and girls play.	Play.
We like to sing.	Like to sing.

Are the words below sentences? Write <u>yes</u> or <u>no</u>.

1. Running. _____

2. A cow laughs. _____

3. A bee and an ant. _____

4. The bugs dance. _____

WRITE AWAY

Look at the words above. Which are not sentences? Add words to make them sentences.

_____

_____

_____

© Houghton Mifflin Harcourt Publishing Company

Name _____ Date _____

Naming Parts

> Every sentence has two parts. The **naming part** tells who or what the sentence is about.
>
> **A frog** hops.
>
> **The snake** crawls.

Write a naming part to complete each sentence.

1. _____ flies.

2. _____ swims.

3. _____ runs.

4. _____ yells.

WRITE AWAY

Get a sheet of paper. Write three naming parts. Ask a friend or family member to add words to make complete sentences.

© Houghton Mifflin Harcourt Publishing Company

Action Parts

> Every sentence has two parts. The **action part** tells what someone or something does.
>
> The girls **kick the ball.**
>
> Lan **paints a picture.**

Write an action part to complete each sentence.

_____

1. Pablo _____

_____

2. The dog _____

_____

3. The soap _____

_____

4. They _____

WRITE AWAY

Get a sheet of paper. Write three action parts. Ask a friend or family member to add words to make complete sentences.

15

Sentence Order

A **sentence** is a group of words. It tells a complete thought. The words must be written in **order** so they make sense.

Mr. Jones has a dog.

The dog ran out the door.

It chased a cat.

Read each group of words. Use them to write a sentence.

1. hissed cat The

_____

- -

_____

2. ran The tree the up cat

_____

- -

_____

3. at dog barked cat The the

_____

- -

_____

WRITE AWAY

Think of a sentence. Then cut a sheet of paper into cards. Write each word of the sentence on a different card. Ask a friend or family member to make a sentence using the cards.

© Houghton Mifflin Harcourt Publishing Company

Telling Sentences

A **telling sentence** is one kind of sentence.

- It tells about something or someone.
- It begins with a capital letter.
- It ends with a **period (.)**.

Jill got her fishing pole**.**

She went to the lake**.**

Write three more telling sentences about the picture.

1. _____

_____

2. _____

_____

3. _____

WRITE AWAY

Get a sheet of paper. Draw a picture of something. Write three clues about it. The clues should be telling sentences. Read the clues to a friend or family member. Have the person guess the picture.

© Houghton Mifflin Harcourt Publishing Company

Asking Sentences

An **asking sentence** is one kind of sentence.

- It asks about something or someone.
- It begins with a capital letter.
- It ends with a **question mark (?)**.

What job do you do**?**

Do you like your job**?**

Write three asking sentences that you could ask a farmer.

1. _____

2. _____

3. _____

WRITE AWAY

Choose a friend or family member that you would like to know more about. Get a sheet of paper. Write three asking sentences. Then ask the person the questions.

© Houghton Mifflin Harcourt Publishing Company

Exclamations

An **exclamation** is one kind of sentence.

- It shows strong feeling and excitement.
- It begins with a capital letter.
- It ends with an **exclamation mark (!)**.

What a big fish you caught**!**

Stop that dog**!**

Look at the picture. Write three exclamations that you could say.

1. _____

2. _____

3. _____

WRITE AWAY

Imagine that you are at a zoo. Get a sheet of paper. Write three exclamations that you might say while you are watching the animals.

© Houghton Mifflin Harcourt Publishing Company

Adding Sense Words

Sense words tell how something looks, smells, tastes, sounds, and feels.

Here are some sense words.

Looks: red, round   Sounds: loud, crunchy

Smells: rotten, sweet   Feels: smooth, hot

Tastes: sweet, sour

Add sense words to each sentence. The first one is done for you.

1. Jed ate a banana.

   Jed ate a mushy, yellow banana.

2. The cat is sleeping.

3. The boy beat the drum.

WRITE AWAY

Get a sheet of paper. Write sentences about an apple.
Use each sense to tell about it.

© Houghton Mifflin Harcourt Publishing Company

Run-on Sentences

A **run-on sentence** has two naming parts and two action parts.

Kim was at the beach she played in the sand.

You can fix a run-on sentence.

- Write two sentences.
- Begin each sentence with a capital letter.
- End each sentence with an end mark.

Kim was at the beach. **S**he played in the sand.

Correct each run-on sentence.

1. She saw a crab it bit her toe.

_____

_____

_____

_____

2. Kim yelled she ran away.

_____

_____

WRITE AWAY

Get a sheet of paper. Correct this very long run-on sentence.

Mia built a sandcastle her dog ran into it the sand flew.

© Houghton Mifflin Harcourt Publishing Company
Core Skills Writing, Grade 1

Writing Sentences

A sentence is a group of words. You should write it using your best handwriting. You should leave a finger space between each word.

Write each sentence. Put spaces between the words. Use your best handwriting.

I. Thedogisdirty.

_____

- -

_____

2. Thegirlgetsatub.

- -

_____

3. Shegivesthedogabath.

_____

- -

_____

WRITE AWAY

What happens when the dog gets a bath?
Get a sheet of paper. Write more sentences.
Tell what happens next.

© Houghton Mifflin Harcourt Publishing Company

Unit 2
Core Skills Writing, Grade 1

Proofreading Sentences

You can proofread sentences. Use **proofreading marks** to look for mistakes. The Proofreading Marks are on page 125.

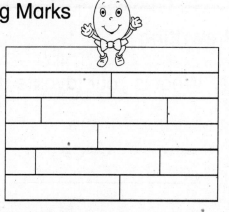

h̲umpty Dumpty sat ∧^{on} a wall⊙

Correct each sentence. Use proofreading marks.
(Hint: Each sentence has two mistakes.)

1. Jack and jill went up a Hill.

2. Little miss Muffet sat on a tuffet

3. Do u know the the muffin man?

WRITE AWAY

Get a sheet of paper. Choose one of the rhymes above.
Write all of the words in the rhyme. Proofread it for mistakes.

23

Name _____   Date _____

Writing: Sentences

It is time to practice using the writing process. Just follow the steps.

Prewriting

1. What is your favorite drink? List three. Circle the one you like most.

_____   _____   _____
- - - - - - - - - - - - - -   - - - - - - - - - - - - - -   - - - - - - - - - - - - - -
_____   _____   _____

2. Write the name of the drink in the middle of the web. Write words about the drink in the outside circles.

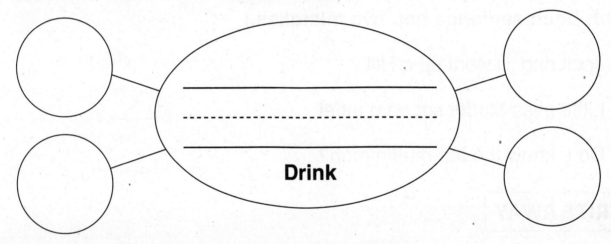

Drink

3. Tell more about the drink. Use sense words.

_____   _____   _____
- - - - - - - - - - - - - -   - - - - - - - - - - - - - -   - - - - - - - - - - - - - -
_____   _____   _____

Looks   Sounds   Tastes

_____   _____
- - - - - - - - - - - - - -   - - - - - - - - - - - - - -
_____   _____

Feels   Smells

© Houghton Mifflin Harcourt Publishing Company

Writing: Sentences, part 2

Drafting

Write sentences about your favorite drink. Use your ideas from prewriting.

_____

- -

_____

- -

_____

- -

_____

- -

_____

- -

_____

- -

_____

- -

_____

- -

_____

- -

_____

- -

_____

- -

_____

© Houghton Mifflin Harcourt Publishing Company

Writing: **Sentences,** part 3

Revising

Look at the sentences in your draft.

- • Do they all make sense?

- • Do they tell about the drink?

- • Do you have enough details?

Share your writing with a partner. Listen to his or her comments.
Write the sentences again. Use another sheet of paper if you need to.

_____

- -

_____

- -

_____

- -

_____

- -

_____

- -

_____

- -

_____

- -

_____

© Houghton Mifflin Harcourt Publishing Company

Writing: Sentences, part 4

Proofreading

Read your sentences three times. Look for a different mistake each time.

- Do all sentences begin with a capital letter?
- Do all sentences have an end mark?
- Are all words spelled correctly?

Use the Proofreading Marks to fix the mistakes on page 26.

≡ Use a capital letter.

/ Use a lowercase letter.

⊙ Add a period.

∧ Add something.

↗ Take out something.

⌃ Change something.

◯ Check the spelling.

Publishing

Now you are ready to share your sentences.

Use a computer or page 28 to publish your work.

- Write a title.
- Write the sentences in your best handwriting. You can also use the tips on page 11 to publish on a computer.
- Draw a picture to go along with your sentences.

© Houghton Mifflin Harcourt Publishing Company

Title _____

_____

_____

_____

_____

_____

_____

_____

_____

_____

_____

_____

© Houghton Mifflin Harcourt Publishing Company

Core Skills Writing, Grade 1

Personal Story

A **personal story** is a special story.

- It tells about something you did or saw.

- It tells how you felt.

- You use the words I, me, and my.

It rained Saturday. I put on my raincoat. I got my umbrella. I went out to play in the rain. It was fun to splash in the water puddles!

Think about something special that you did or saw. Draw a picture to show what happened.

WRITE AWAY

Write a sentence to tell what is happening in your picture.

_____

- -

_____

_____

- -

_____

© Houghton Mifflin Harcourt Publishing Company

Name _____ Date _____

Naming Words

Some words name people. Some words name places or things. These are **naming words.**

My **dad** can sing.   (person)

The **store** opens soon.   (place)

The **milk** is cold.   (thing)

Look at each picture. Write if it is a <u>person</u>, <u>place</u>, or <u>thing</u>.

1.

2.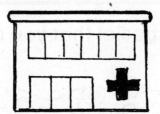

3.

_____   _____   _____
- - - - - - - - -   - - - - - - - - -   - - - - - - - - -
_____   _____   _____

WRITE AWAY

Look around you. Write the name of a person, place, or thing that you see.

person   place   thing

_____   _____   _____
- - - - - - - - -   - - - - - - - - -   - - - - - - - - -
_____   _____   _____

© Houghton Mifflin Harcourt Publishing Company

Name _____ Date _____

Special Naming Words

A **naming word** is a person, place, or thing.
Some naming words are special people, places,
or things. They begin with a capital letter.

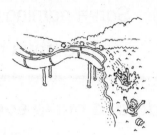

Ellen Lee packs a picnic.   (special person)

She goes to **West Water Park.**   (special place)

Ellen will ride the **Wet and Wild Slide.**   (special thing)

Answer the questions. Use special naming words.

1. What is the name of your street?

_____

- -

_____

2. What is your friend's name?

_____

- -

_____

3. What is the name of your favorite board game?

_____

- -

_____

WRITE AWAY

Think about a time you went to visit someone special. Get a sheet of
paper. Draw a picture of yourself with this person. Write a personal story
about the visit. Use two special naming words.

© Houghton Mifflin Harcourt Publishing Company

Naming Words That End in s

Some naming words tell about more than one. They end in s.

The **boys** ride **bikes**.

Add s to make each word mean more than one.

1.   ball _____

2. 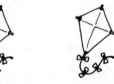 kite _____

3.   bear _____

4.   car _____

WRITE AWAY

What is your favorite toy? Get a sheet of paper. Draw a picture of yourself with the toy. Then write a personal story about the picture. Use two naming words that tell about more than one.

© Houghton Mifflin Harcourt Publishing Company

Naming Words That End in <u>es</u>

> Some naming words tell about more than one. They end in <u>es</u>. Look for words that end in <u>x</u>, <u>ch</u>, <u>sh</u>, or <u>ss</u>.
>
> The **fox<u>es</u>** eat **peach<u>es</u>.**

Add <u>es</u> to make each word mean more than one.

1.  dish

_____

2. 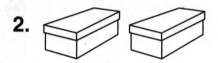 box

_____

3. dress

_____

4. wrench

_____

WRITE AWAY

Think about your birthday. Get a sheet of paper. Draw a picture of yourself with the wrapped boxes. Then write a personal story about what you got. Use two naming words that end in <u>es</u>.

© Houghton Mifflin Harcourt Publishing Company

Drawing a Picture

Draw a picture of what you did or saw before you write a personal story. The picture will help you think of what to put in your story.

Think about something funny that happened to you. Draw a picture of the most important part.

WRITE AWAY

Get a sheet of paper. Write a personal story to tell about the funny thing that happened.

© Houghton Mifflin Harcourt Publishing Company   Core Skills Writing, Grade 1

Telling About One Idea

A personal story tells about something you did or saw. It should tell about only one idea.

Cat will write a personal story about his day outside with Rabbit. He drew pictures to show what he will tell. Cross out the picture that he should not tell about.

WRITE AWAY

Get a sheet of paper. Then imagine that you are Hippo. Write a personal story about going to the beach. Remember to use the words <u>I</u>, <u>me</u>, and <u>my</u>.

© Houghton Mifflin Harcourt Publishing Company

The First Sentence

A **main idea** is the most important idea. Tell the main idea in the first sentence of your personal story.

Look at each picture. Circle the sentence that tells the main idea.

1.

Lita and I played a game.

It was too cold to go outside.

2.

I swam with my friend today.

I swam really fast.

3.

The ball flew into the air.

I played soccer with my friends.

WRITE AWAY

Get a sheet of paper. Draw a picture of something you did with a friend. Then write a personal story about it. Write the main idea in the first sentence.

© Houghton Mifflin Harcourt Publishing Company

Name _____ Date _____

Important Details

Write important **details** in a personal story.
- Tell <u>who</u> is in the story.
- Tell <u>where</u> the story happens.
- Tell <u>what</u> happens.

Think about a special place you visited. Get a sheet of paper. Draw a picture to show something that happened at the special place. Then write the details.

Who _____

_____

Where _____

_____

What _____

_____

_____

| WRITE AWAY |

Get a sheet of paper. Write a personal story that tells about your picture.

© Houghton Mifflin Harcourt Publishing Company

Story Order

A personal story can tell about something you did. You should tell what you did in **order.**

Look at each picture. Then write numbers 1, 2, and 3 to show how you would order them.

1.

2.

3.

_____   _____   _____
- - - - - - - - - - - - - - - -   - - - - - - - - - - - - - - - -   - - - - - - - - - - - - - - - -
_____   _____   _____

WRITE AWAY

Get a sheet of paper. Think about a time that something funny happened when you got ready for school. Write a personal story about it.

© Houghton Mifflin Harcourt Publishing Company

Name _____ Date _____

Talking to a Friend

> When you write, pretend you are talking to a friend. Use the same words you would say. It helps the writing sound like you.

Think about a time you played in water.
What would you tell a friend about it?
Write two sentences that use your own words.

1. _____

_____

_____

2. _____

_____

_____

WRITE AWAY

Get a sheet of paper. Write a personal story that tells about the time you played in water. Make the sentences sound like you are talking to a friend.

© Houghton Mifflin Harcourt Publishing Company

Writing: Personal Story

It is time to use the writing process. You will write a **personal story.** Just follow the steps.

Prewriting

1. What is something special you have done? List two ideas.

   _____

   _____

   _____
   ----

2. Choose the idea that you like best. Circle it.

3. What details will you write in the story?

   _____

   Who _____
   _____

   Where _____
   _____

   What _____
   _____

   _____

4. Get a sheet of paper. Draw a picture of the most important part.

© Houghton Mifflin Harcourt Publishing Company

Writing: Personal Story, part 2

5. What happened in the story? Tell the order.

First,

Then,

Next,

Then,

Finally,

6. Write a sentence that will be the last sentence in the paragraph. It is like the first sentence but with different words.

_____

- -

_____

© Houghton Mifflin Harcourt Publishing Company

Writing: Personal Story, part 3

Drafting

Write a draft of your personal story. Use your ideas from prewriting.

_____

- -

_____

- -

_____

- -

_____

- -

_____

- -

_____

- -

_____

- -

_____

- -

_____

- -

_____

- -

_____

- -

_____

© Houghton Mifflin Harcourt Publishing Company

Writing: Personal Story, part 4

Revising

Look at the sentences in your draft.

- Does your first sentence tell the main idea?

- Do you tell all the details?

- Do you tell what happened in order?

- Do your sentences sound like you are talking to a friend?

- Is your last sentence like your first sentence but with different words?

Share your writing with a partner. Listen to his or her comments. Write the sentences again. Use another sheet of paper if you need to.

_____

- -

_____

- -

_____

- -

_____

- -

_____

- -

_____

© Houghton Mifflin Harcourt Publishing Company

Name _____ Date _____

Writing: Personal Story, part 5

Proofreading
Read your personal story three times. Look for a
different mistake each time.

Read for capital letters.

- Do all sentences begin with a
  capital letter?

- Do all special names begin with a
  capital letter?

- Does the word I have a capital letter?

Read for end marks.

- Do all sentences have an end mark?

Read for spelling.

- Are all words spelled correctly?

Use the Proofreading Marks to fix the mistakes on page 43.

Publishing
Now you are ready to share your personal story.
Use a computer or page 45 to publish your work.

- Write a title.

- Write your personal story in your best handwriting.
  You can also use the tips on page 11 to publish
  on a computer.

- Get a large sheet of construction paper. Paste
  your story on one side. Paste your picture beside it.

≡	Use a capital letter.
/	Use a lowercase letter.
⊙	Add a period.
∧	Add something.
℘	Take out something.
∧	Change something.
○	Check the spelling.

© Houghton Mifflin Harcourt Publishing Company

Unit 3
Core Skills Writing, Grade 1

Name _____ Date _____

Title _____

© Houghton Mifflin Harcourt Publishing Company

Friendly Letter

You send a **friendly letter** to someone you know. A friendly letter has five parts.

heading — May 5, 2013

greeting — Dear Grandma,

body — Mom and I went to the zoo. We saw a baby seal. It was just born. We had lots of fun.

closing — Love,

signature — Leon

Who could you send a friendly letter to?
Write the name in the greeting.

_____

Dear _____,

| WRITE AWAY |

How would you end the letter? Write a closing and signature.

_____

- -

_____

- -

_____

© Houghton Mifflin Harcourt Publishing Company

Action Words

> An **action word** tells what someone or something does.
>
> The dog **barks.**
>
> The girls **laugh.**

What is happening in each picture? Write an action word from the box.

| eat | read | sleep |

1.

2.

3.

WRITE AWAY

Ask a friend or family member to write sentences with action words on a sheet of paper. Tell him or her to make three mistakes. Find the mistakes and correct them using the Proofreading Marks on page 125.

© Houghton Mifflin Harcourt Publishing Company

Action Words for Now

An **action word** can tell what someone or something does now.

- Add <u>s</u> to an action word that tells about one person, place, or thing.
- Don't add anything to an action word that tells about more than one person, place, or thing.

The horse **runs**.   The horses **run**.

Complete each sentence. Write an action word to show the action that is happening now.

1. A cow _____

_____

2. Three goats _____

WRITE AWAY

The word <u>fish</u> can name one and more than one. Write a sentence that tells something one fish does now. Then write a sentence that tells what two fish do now.

_____

_____

_____

_____

© Houghton Mifflin Harcourt Publishing Company

Action Words for the Past

An **action word** can tell what someone or something did in the past. Add <u>ed</u> to these words.

Andy **helps** his sister.   (now)

Andy **helped** his sister last week.   (happened in the past)

Look at the picture. Write two sentences.
Use action words that happened in the past.

1. _____

_____

2. _____

WRITE AWAY

Write a sentence to tell what you did yesterday.

_____

_____

_____

_____

_____

© Houghton Mifflin Harcourt Publishing Company

Action Words That Change Spellings

An **action word** can tell what someone or something did in the past. Many action words end in ed. Some action words change their spellings.

The girls **see** a fish.   (now)

The girls **saw** a fish yesterday.   (happened in the past)

Read each sentence. Circle the word that completes the sentence.

1. John (swims, swam) in the lake now.

2. John (swims, swam) in the lake yesterday, too.

3. John (takes, took) his tube yesterday.

4. Today John (takes, took) his tube.

| WRITE AWAY |

Write two sentences. Use the words run and ran.

_____

- -

_____

- -

_____

© Houghton Mifflin Harcourt Publishing Company

Exact Action Words

Action words tell how someone or something moves. The best action words tell exactly how they move.

The dog **runs** after the cat.

The dog **races** after the cat.

Look at each <u>underlined</u> word. Choose an exact action word to take its place. Write the sentence with the new word.

I. The rabbit <u>has</u> a carrot.

_____

- -

_____

2. The turtle <u>walks</u> to the pond.

_____

- -

_____

WRITE AWAY

Read the sentence below. Write two exact words that could take the place of <u>eat</u>.

The cows eat grass.

_____

- -

_____

© Houghton Mifflin Harcourt Publishing Company

Months and Days

The names of months and days are special words. They begin with a capital letter.

Today is **Monday.**

My birthday is in **July.**

Answer the questions. Begin each with a capital letter.

1. What is today? _____

2. What month is it? _____

3. What month is your birthday? _____

WRITE AWAY

What is your favorite day? Why do you like this day? Get a sheet of paper. Write a letter to a family member telling why this day is your favorite.

52

Unit 4
Core Skills Writing, Grade 1

Commas

You will use a **comma** (,) when you write letters.

- Write a comma in the **heading** after the day.
- Write a comma after the **greeting.**
- Write a comma after the **closing.**

heading — October 18, 2014

greeting — Dear José,

body — I got a new cat. I named him Buttons.

closing — Your friend,

signature — Lisa

Read the letter. Write the missing commas.

October 25 2014

Dear Lisa

I am coming to visit next month. I can't wait to meet Buttons.

Sincerely

José

WRITE AWAY

Think about a pet that does something funny.
The pet can belong to you or a neighbor. Then get a sheet
of paper. Write a letter to a family member telling what the pet does.

© Houghton Mifflin Harcourt Publishing Company

The Reader

The **reader** is the person who reads your words. You need to tell the reader things that the person will want to know about.

Pretend that you are at a summer camp. You will write some letters home. Look at the name of each reader. What will you tell the person about camp?

_____

- -

1. Mother _____

- -

_____

- -

2. Friend _____

- -

_____

WRITE AWAY

Get a sheet of paper. Choose one person above.

Then write a letter to that person.

Tell the person about the camp.

54

A Fun First Sentence

Make the first sentence in a letter fun. Then the reader will want to keep reading.

It rained.   (not fun)   It rained cats and dogs.   (fun)

Jun went home.   (not fun)   Jun skipped home happily.   (fun)

Read each sentence. Write it a new way. Make it more fun.

1. I flew a kite.

_____

- -

_____

2. Dad made a pie.

_____

- -

_____

WRITE AWAY

Get a sheet of paper. Think of something good that happened today. Write a letter to a family member. Tell the person what happened. Make the first sentence fun.

© Houghton Mifflin Harcourt Publishing Company

Name _____   Date _____

Sentence Beginnings

Some sentences can begin with the same words. You can change the words to make your writing fun to read. Use these words: I, you, he, she, it, we, and they.

Anna has a garden. **Anna** grows flowers.

Anna has a garden. **She** grows flowers.

Read the sentences. Write the second sentence a different way. Use a different beginning.

I. Anna worked in the garden. Anna watered the flowers.

_____

- -

_____

2. The flowers are yellow. The flowers are tall.

_____

- -

_____

3. Tom wants a flower. Tom picks a flower.

_____

- -

_____

WRITE AWAY

What would you grow in a garden? Get a sheet of paper. Then write a letter to Anna. Tell her what you would like to grow.

56

Writing: Friendly Letter

It is time to use the writing process. You will write a **friendly letter.** Just follow the steps.

Prewriting

1. Who would you like to write to?

_____

_____

2. What would you like to write about? List three ideas.

_____

_____

_____

_____

_____

3. Which idea would the person like to know about? Circle it.

4. What interesting first sentence can you write?

_____

_____

_____

_____

© Houghton Mifflin Harcourt Publishing Company

Name _____ Date _____

Writing: Friendly Letter, part 2

Drafting

Write a draft of your friendly letter. Use your ideas from prewriting.

_____

- -

(Heading) _____

_____

- -

(Greeting) Dear _____

_____

- -

_____

- -

_____

- -

_____

- -

_____

- -

_____

- -

(Closing) _____

_____

- -

(Signature) _____

© Houghton Mifflin Harcourt Publishing Company

Writing: Friendly Letter, part 3

Revising

Look at the sentences in your draft.

- Do you tell the reader something interesting?

- Is your first sentence fun?

- Do the action words tell about the past?

- Do you use exact action words?

- Do you use different words at the beginning of sentences?

Write your letter again.

_____

- -

_____

_____

- -

Dear _____

_____

- -

_____

_____

- -

_____

_____

- -

_____

_____

- -

_____

_____

- -

_____

59

Writing: Friendly Letter, part 4

Proofreading

Read your friendly letter three times. Look for a different mistake each time.

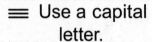

> | | |
> |---|---|
> | ≡ | Use a capital letter. |
> | / | Use a lowercase letter. |
> | ⊙ | Add a period. |
> | ∧ | Add something. |
> | ✌ | Take out something. |
> | ⋏ | Change something. |
> | ◯ | Check the spelling. |

Read for capital letters.

- Do all sentences begin with a capital letter?
- Do all special names begin with a capital letter?

Read for end marks and commas.

- Do the names of months and dates begin with a capital letter?
- Does the word I have a capital letter?
- Do all sentences have an end mark?
- Is there a comma in the date?
- Is there a comma after the greeting and closing?

Read for spelling and the parts of a letter.

- Are all words spelled correctly?
- Does the letter have all five parts?

Use the Proofreading Marks to fix the mistakes on page 59.

Publishing

- Now you are ready to share your letter.
- Use a computer or page 61 to publish your work.
- Write the letter in your best handwriting. You can also use the tips on page 11 to publish on a computer. Then ask a family member to help you mail your letter!

© Houghton Mifflin Harcourt Publishing Company

Name _____ Date _____

_____

_____

Dear _____

_____

_____

_____

_____

_____

_____

_____

_____

_____

_____

_____

_____

© Houghton Mifflin Harcourt Publishing Company

Description

> A **description** tells about a person, place, or thing. You use **details** to tell about it. The details help the reader see what you see.
>
> I saw a rabbit in the garden. It was brown. It had long ears and a white fluffy tail. The rabbit was eating carrots.

Look at the description above.
Write three details about the rabbit.

1. _____

2. _____

3. _____

WRITE AWAY

Get a sheet of paper. Choose another animal. Write a description of it.

© Houghton Mifflin Harcourt Publishing Company

Name _____ Date _____

Describing Words

> **Describing words** tell what a person, place, or thing is like.
> The **white** kitten plays with a **little** ball.

Color the picture. Write describing words to tell about it.

_____

_____ hair

_____

_____ eyes

_____

_____ horns

_____

_____ teeth

WRITE AWAY

Get a sheet of paper. Write a description of the picture.

63

© Houghton Mifflin Harcourt Publishing Company

Unit 5
Core Skills Writing, Grade 1

Telling How Something Looks

A **describing word** can tell how something looks. It can tell about size and color. It can tell about shape and how many there are.

The **pink** flower is **tall.**

Pat has **three round** cookies.

Complete the sentences. Write describing words.

_____

\- -

1. Pete had a _____ kite.

(shape)

_____

\- -

2. He bought a _____ kite.

(size)

_____

\- -

3. His new kite was _____

(color)

_____

\- -

4. Pete had _____ kites to fly.

(number)

WRITE AWAY

Get a sheet of paper. Draw a picture of a kite that you would like to have. Then write a description of it.

64

Telling How Something Tastes and Smells

A **describing word** can tell how something tastes. It can tell how something smells, too.

The apple pie smelled **spicy.** (smell)

It was **sweet,** too. (taste)

Look at each picture. Write a describing word that tells how each tastes and smells.

	Taste	Smell
1.		
2.		
3.		
4.		

WRITE AWAY

Get a sheet of paper. Choose one picture above. Then write a description of it.

© Houghton Mifflin Harcourt Publishing Company

Unit 5
Core Skills Writing, Grade 1

Telling How Something Sounds and Feels

A **describing word** can tell how something sounds. It can tell how something feels, too.

The **hot** dog gave a **loud** bark.

↑ (feel)　　　　↑ (sound)

Look at each picture. Write a describing word that tells how each sounds and feels.

	Sound	Feel
1.	_____	_____
2.	_____	_____
3.	_____	_____
4.	_____	_____

WRITE AWAY

Get a sheet of paper. Choose one picture above. Then write a description of it.

© Houghton Mifflin Harcourt Publishing Company

Telling About Feelings

A **describing word** can tell how a person feels.

The girls were **happy.**

Gloria was **surprised.**

Look at each picture. Write a describing word that tells how the person feels.

1.

_____

- - - - - - - - - - - - - - - -

2.

_____

- - - - - - - - - - - - - - - -

3.

_____

- - - - - - - - - - - - - - - -

4.

_____

- - - - - - - - - - - - - - - -

5.

_____

- - - - - - - - - - - - - - - -

6.

_____

- - - - - - - - - - - - - - - -

WRITE AWAY

Get a sheet of paper. Choose one picture above. Describe a time when you felt this way.

© Houghton Mifflin Harcourt Publishing Company

Joining Sentences with the Same Naming Part

You can join sentences that have the same naming part. Use the word <u>and</u> between the action parts.

John ran. **John** played.

John ran <u>and</u> played.

Join each pair of sentences. Write one sentence.

1. John sat down. John rested.

_____

- -

_____

2. John ate an apple. John ate honey.

_____

- -

_____

3. He saw a bee. He saw a kitten.

_____

- -

_____

| WRITE AWAY |

What else did John do? Get a sheet of paper. Write sentences that tell more about John. Look for sentences that you can join. Tell a friend or family member how you could join the short sentences.

© Houghton Mifflin Harcourt Publishing Company

Name _____ Date _____

Joining Sentences with the Same Action Part

You can join sentences that have the same action part. Use the word <u>and</u> between the naming parts.

Jan **had a birthday party.** Ann **had a birthday party.**

Jan <u>and</u> Ann **had a birthday party.**

Join each pair of sentences. Write one sentence.

1. Jed came to the party. Ed came to the party.

_____

- -

_____

2. Jan got presents. Ann got presents.

_____

- -

_____

3. The girls played games. The boys played games.

_____

- -

_____

WRITE AWAY

What else did the children do at the party? Get a sheet of paper. Write sentences that tell more about the party. Look for sentences that you can join. Tell a friend or family member how you could join the sentences.

© Houghton Mifflin Harcourt Publishing Company

Name _____ Date _____

Joining Sentences to List Words

Sometimes you can join sentences to make a list. The sentences have parts that are the same. You use the word <u>and</u>. You write a **comma (,)** between the words in the list.

Jill <u>sang</u>. **Ling** <u>sang</u>. **Ron** <u>sang</u>.

Jill, Ling, <u>and</u> **Ron** <u>sang</u>.

<u>Jill took a</u> **dress**. <u>Jill took a</u> **coat**. <u>Jill took a</u> **hat**.

<u>Jill took a</u> **dress, coat,** and **hat**.

Combine each set of sentences. Write one sentence.

1. Eva called Jen. Eva called Jo. Eva called Tom.

_____

- -

_____

2. Rabbit will go. Bear will go. Kitten will go.

_____

- -

_____

WRITE AWAY

What did you eat today? Write one sentence that lists three foods.

_____

- -

_____

- -

_____

© Houghton Mifflin Harcourt Publishing Company

Short and Long Sentences

When you write, you should write short and long sentences. They make your writing more interesting.

The lion got caught in a net. The lion roared for help. The mouse ran to help. The mouse chewed the net. The lion was free.

The lion got caught in a net and roared for help. The mouse ran to help. Then the mouse chewed the net. The lion was free.

Read the story. Write it a different way. Write sentences that have different lengths.

Fox was hungry. Fox looked for food. Fox saw some grapes. The grapes were high. Fox was not happy. Fox left.

_____

- -

_____

- -

_____

- -

WRITE AWAY

Get a sheet of paper. Look at the story above. Write it a different way.

© Houghton Mifflin Harcourt Publishing Company

Adding Details

You should write lots of **details**. They tell more about your idea. They make your writing more fun.

The baby cried.

The **sad** baby cried **loudly in the store.**

Write each sentence again. Add at least two details.

1. Howard dug a hole.

_____

_____

_____

2. He found a box.

_____

_____

_____

WRITE AWAY

Get a sheet of paper. Tell more about the box Howard found. Give lots of details.

© Houghton Mifflin Harcourt Publishing Company

Words That Paint a Picture

You can use words to paint a picture. You can write about two things that are alike. You **compare** them.

The **room** was as hot as **an oven.**

The room is compared to a hot oven. The sentence tells that the room is very hot.

Read each word picture. Underline the two things that are being compared. Then tell how they are alike.

1. John's feet smelled like stinky garbage.

_____

- -

_____

2. The children ran as fast as rabbits.

_____

- -

_____

WRITE AWAY

Finish the sentence below. Add words to help paint a picture.

_____

- -

The pillow _____

© Houghton Mifflin Harcourt Publishing Company

Main Idea and Details

The **main idea** is what you are writing about. The **details** tell more about the main idea. A **web** can help you think of details.

What is your favorite food? Write the name of the food in the middle of the web. Write details about it in the outside circles.

WRITE AWAY

Get a sheet of paper. Describe your favorite food.

© Houghton Mifflin Harcourt Publishing Company

Name _____ Date _____

What Is a Paragraph?

> A **paragraph** is a group of sentences. The first sentence tells about one main idea. The other sentences give details about the main idea.
>
> The first line is **indented.** This means that the first word is moved one finger space to the right.
>
> Rosa saw three eggs in a nest. The eggs were light blue. They had little brown spots on them. A wren laid those eggs.

Look at the picture. Write a paragraph about it.

_____

- -

_____

- -

_____

- -

_____

WRITE AWAY

Read your paragraph. Can you make it better? Get a sheet of paper. Then write your paragraph again.

75

Choosing a Title

You need to write a **title** for your work. A title is the name you give your writing.

- Think about the main idea.
- Look for words that are repeated.
- Begin the first word with a capital letter.
- Important words begin with a capital letter. These words do not: <u>a</u>, <u>an</u>, <u>the</u>, <u>for</u>, <u>at</u>, and <u>in</u>.

Read the titles of the nursery rhymes below.
Write titles that are more interesting.

1. Humpty Dumpty _____

_____

2. Jack and Jill _____

_____

3. Little Boy Blue _____

WRITE AWAY

What is the title of your favorite book? Get a sheet of paper. Tell if it is a good title or not. Tell why or why not.

© Houghton Mifflin Harcourt Publishing Company

Name _____ Date _____

Writing: Description

It is time to use the writing process. You will write a **description**. Just follow the steps.

Prewriting

1. What would you like to describe? Think about people, places, and things. List three ideas.

_____
- -
_____
_____
- -
_____
_____
- -
_____

2. Which idea could you describe the best? Circle it.

3. Draw a picture of what you will describe. Add lots of details.

© Houghton Mifflin Harcourt Publishing Company

Writing: Description, part 2

4. Write your idea in the middle of the web. Write details about it in the outside circles. Add more circles if you need to.

© Houghton Mifflin Harcourt Publishing Company

Writing: Description, part 3

Drafting

Write a draft of your description. Use your ideas from prewriting.

_____

- -

_____

- -

_____

- -

_____

- -

_____

- -

_____

- -

_____

- -

_____

- -

_____

© Houghton Mifflin Harcourt Publishing Company

Writing: Description, part 4

Revising

Look at the sentences in your draft.

- Do you use describing words that tell more about how something looks, tastes, smells, sounds, and feels?
- Can you join some sentences?
- Do you have long and short sentences?
- Do you use words that paint a picture?
- Do the sentences make a paragraph?

Share your writing with a partner. Listen to his or her comments. Write your description again. Use another sheet of paper if you need to.

_____

- -

_____

- -

_____

- -

_____

- -

_____

- -

_____

- -

_____

- -

_____

© Houghton Mifflin Harcourt Publishing Company

Writing: Description, part 5

Proofreading

Read your description three times. Look for a different mistake each time.

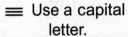

≡	Use a capital letter.
/	Use a lowercase letter.
⊙	Add a period.
∧	Add something.
℘	Take out something.
⌃	Change something.
○	Check the spelling.

Read for capital letters.

- Do all sentences begin with a capital letter?

- Do all special names begin with a capital letter?

Read for end marks and commas.

- Is there a comma when three or more things are listed?

- Do all sentences have an end mark?

Read for spelling and spaces.

- Is the first word in the paragraph indented?

- Are all words spelled correctly?

Use the Proofreading Marks to fix the mistakes on page 80.

Publishing

Now you are ready to share your description. Use a computer or page 82 to publish your work.

- Write a title.

- Write your description in your best handwriting. You can also use the tips on page II to publish on a computer.

- Get a large sheet of construction paper. Paste your description on one side. Paste the picture you drew beside it.

© Houghton Mifflin Harcourt Publishing Company

Name _____ Date _____

_____

Title _____

_____

_____

_____

_____

_____

_____

_____

_____

_____

_____

_____

_____

_____

_____

_____

82

© Houghton Mifflin Harcourt Publishing Company

How-to Paragraph

A **how-to paragraph** tells how to make or do something. It lists the things you will use. It lists the steps in order, too. Li reads a how-to book about planting seeds. This is what she wrote.

How to Plant Flower Seeds

Planting flower seeds is fun. You will need seeds, a shovel, and water. First, dig a hole. Then, put seeds in the hole and cover them up. Finally, water the seeds. The seeds will grow quickly!

Answer the questions.

1. What is the paragraph telling you to do?

_____

- -

_____

2. What things do you need?

_____

- -

_____

3. What do you do before you cover the seeds?

_____

- -

_____

WRITE AWAY

Get a sheet of paper. Write what the first and last steps are when you plant seeds.

© Houghton Mifflin Harcourt Publishing Company

Writing Steps

A **how-to paragraph** tells how to make or do something.
You can use a chart to help you write the steps in order.

**What is your favorite sandwich? Tell how to
make it. Write one step in each box.**

First,

↓

_____,

↓

_____,

↓

Finally,

WRITE AWAY

Work with a partner. Find a how-to book. Read the book together. What
did you learn how to do? Get a sheet of paper. Write the steps in order.

© Houghton Mifflin Harcourt Publishing Company

Name _____ Date _____

Time-Order Words

A **how-to paragraph** tells how to make or do something. The steps must be in order. **Time-order words** can help you tell when something happens.

first   then   next   soon   after   before   finally

Look at the pictures. Write a time-order word to tell the steps in order.

_____
- -
_____, a bird builds a nest.

_____
- -
_____, the bird lays eggs.

_____
- -
_____, the baby birds hatch.

WRITE AWAY

Choose a how-to book. Read it with a partner. What did you learn how to do? Talk about the steps. Get a sheet of paper. Write a how-to paragraph. Use time-order words.

© Houghton Mifflin Harcourt Publishing Company

Name _____ Date _____

Direction Words

Direction words tell where something is. They tell where to place things.

over   under   in   out   on   through   by

Look at the picture. Complete the sentence to tell where the mouse went.

The mouse ran

_____

- -

over the _____,

_____

- -

around the _____,

_____

- -

over the _____,

_____

- -

and down the _____.

WRITE AWAY

Where else did the mouse run? Get a sheet of paper. Write more sentences. Circle the direction words you use.

© Houghton Mifflin Harcourt Publishing Company

Words with Like Meanings

A **word with a like meaning** is a word that means almost the same as another word.

Leo was **happy.**

Leo was **glad.**

Write each sentence again. Use a word with a like meaning from the box.

raced	tall	angry

1. Raccoon climbed a <u>big</u> tree.

_____

- -

_____

2. He saw some <u>mad</u> bees.

_____

- -

_____

3. Raccoon <u>ran</u> away from the bees.

_____

- -

_____

WRITE AWAY

Think of more words that have the same meaning. Get a sheet of paper. Write as many words as you can.

© Houghton Mifflin Harcourt Publishing Company

Words with Opposite Meanings

A **word with an opposite meaning** is a word that means the opposite of another word.

walk/run   fast/slow   tall/short

Look at each picture. Write a word from the box that has an opposite meaning.

cold   dry   close   dirty

1.

_____

- - - - - - - - - - - - - - - - - -

_____

3.

_____

- - - - - - - - - - - - - - - - - -

_____

2.

_____

- - - - - - - - - - - - - - - - - -

_____

4.

_____

- - - - - - - - - - - - - - - - - -

_____

WRITE AWAY

Think of more words that have opposite meanings. Get a sheet of paper. Write as many words as you can that have opposite meanings.

© Houghton Mifflin Harcourt Publishing Company

Unit 6
Core Skills Writing, Grade 1

Words That Sound Alike

Some words sound alike, but they have different spellings. They have different meanings, too.

Turtle **one** the race.

Turtle **won** the race.

<u>One</u> is a number. <u>Won</u> means "to have done the best." The right sentence is <u>Turtle won the race</u>.

Circle the word that has the right meaning.

1. Lisa is going (to, too, two) the pet store.

2. She wants to (by, buy) some fish.

3. She (seas, sees) lots of fish.

4. Lisa will buy (four, for) fish today.

WRITE AWAY

The words <u>red</u> and <u>read</u> are tricky words. Write a sentence using each word correctly.

_____

- -

_____

_____

- -

_____

© Houghton Mifflin Harcourt Publishing Company

Writing Good Directions

A **how-to paragraph** tells how to make or do something. You need to give good directions. They will help someone do the task.

Look at the pictures. They tell how to make a whale puppet. Write good directions.

1. _____

   _____

2. _____

   _____

3. _____

   _____

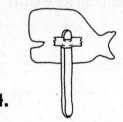

4. _____

   _____

WRITE AWAY

Get a sheet of paper. Write directions telling how to make something you learned from a book.

© Houghton Mifflin Harcourt Publishing Company

Writing an Ending Sentence

The **ending sentence** is the last sentence in a paragraph. It is like the first sentence, but you use different words.

There is an easy way to blow up a balloon. You will need one balloon. First, stretch the balloon. Then, blow into it. Finally, tie a knot in the opening. **Blowing up a balloon is easy.**

Answer the questions.

1. What is the first sentence?

_____

_____

_____

_____

2. What is the last sentence?

_____

_____

WRITE AWAY

How do you put on a shirt? Get a sheet of paper. Write a how-to paragraph. Write an ending sentence that is like the first sentence but uses different words.

91

© Houghton Mifflin Harcourt Publishing Company

Where to Put Pictures

Some steps may be hard to tell in a **how-to paragraph.**
A picture can help tell a step. Put the picture near the words.

Read the steps. Draw a line to show where to put the pictures.

1. Cut the gift-wrap paper.

a.

2. Put the paper around the box.

b.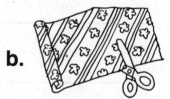

3. Put tape on the paper.

c.

4. Tape a bow to the gift.

d.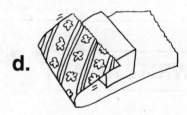

WRITE AWAY

Who could you wrap a gift for? Get a sheet of paper. Write the names of
two people you would wrap a gift for.

© Houghton Mifflin Harcourt Publishing Company

Friendly Help

Ask a friend to read your **how-to paragraph.** Your friend can tell you which steps are not good. Then you can write the steps again to make them better.

Read the how-to paragraph Tonya wrote.
How could she make it better? Write two ideas.

I can play hide-and-seek. You can, too.
You will need room to hide. You also need some
friends. Count so your friends can hide. Then go and find them.

1. _____

_____

_____

_____

2. _____

_____

_____

WRITE AWAY

What game do you like to play? Get a sheet of paper. Write a how-to paragraph that gives the steps. Ask a friend to read it and tell how to make the steps better.

93

Writing: How-to Paragraph

It is time to use the writing process. You will write a **how-to paragraph.** Just follow the steps.

Prewriting

1. Think about the how-to books you read. What did you learn how to do or make? List three ideas.

_____

_____

_____

2. In which ideas can you name all the steps? Circle them with a blue crayon.

3. In which ideas can you tell each step well? Circle them with a red crayon.

4. Think about the idea that you can tell about best. Write the name of the one that you will tell about.

_____

_____

© Houghton Mifflin Harcourt Publishing Company   Unit 6
                                                    Core Skills Writing, Grade 1

Writing: How-to Paragraph, part 2

5. Write the steps to do or make what you choose.
Put them in order. The chart will help you.

First,

↓

_____,

↓

_____,

↓

_____,

↓

Finally,

6. Where can you put pictures? Write your ideas next to the steps in the chart.

© Houghton Mifflin Harcourt Publishing Company

Writing: How-to Paragraph, part 3

Drafting

Write a draft of your how-to paragraph. Use your ideas from prewriting.

_____

- -
_____
- -
_____
- -
_____
- -
_____
- -
_____
- -
_____
- -
_____
- -
_____
- -
_____
- -
_____
- -
_____

© Houghton Mifflin Harcourt Publishing Company

Writing: How-to Paragraph, part 4

Revising

Look at the sentences in your draft.

- Are the steps in order?

- Do you use time-order words?

- Do you use direction words?

- Do you have an ending sentence?

- Is your ending sentence different from the first sentence?

- Has a friend read your paragraph to see if the steps are good?

Share your writing with a partner. Listen to his or her comments. Write your how-to paragraph again. Use another sheet of paper if you need to.

_____

- -

_____

- -

_____

- -

_____

- -

_____

- -

_____

- -

_____

© Houghton Mifflin Harcourt Publishing Company

Writing: How-to Paragraph, part 5

Proofreading

Read your how-to paragraph three times.
Look for a different mistake each time.

≡	Use a capital letter.
/	Use a lowercase letter.
⊙	Add a period.
∧	Add something.
✐	Take out something.
⋀	Change something.
○	Check the spelling.

Read for capital letters.

- Do all sentences begin with a capital letter?

Read for end marks and commas.

- Is there a comma when three or more things are listed?

- Do all sentences have an end mark?

Read for spelling and spaces.

- Is the first word indented in the paragraph?

- Are all words spelled correctly?

Use the Proofreading Marks to fix the mistakes on page 97.

Publishing

Now you are ready to share your how-to paragraph.
Use a computer or page 99 to publish your work.

- Write a title.

- Write your how-to paragraph in your best handwriting. You can also use the tips on page 11 to publish on a computer.

- Draw your pictures.

- Get a large sheet of construction paper. Paste your paragraph and pictures on it.

© Houghton Mifflin Harcourt Publishing Company

Name _____ Date _____

_____

- -

Title _____

_____

- -

_____

- -

_____

- -

_____

- -

_____

- -

_____

- -

_____

- -

_____

- -

_____

- -

_____

99

© Houghton Mifflin Harcourt Publishing Company

Information Paragraph

An **information paragraph** gives **facts** and details about one thing. A fact is something that can happen.

Frog Legs

A frog has long legs that help it stay safe. The legs help it jump on land. The legs help it swim in water. The frog uses its legs to hop and swim away from animals that will eat it.

Answer the questions.

1. What is the paragraph mostly about?

   _____
   -
   _____

2. What is one fact in the paragraph?

   _____
   -
   _____
   -
   _____

WRITE AWAY

Get a sheet of paper. Write two facts about a fish.

© Houghton Mifflin Harcourt Publishing Company

Fact or Fantasy?

Some stories that you read give **facts.** A fact tells about something that can really happen. Some stories you read tell about things that cannot happen. These stories are called **fantasy.**

Benny Bee is a worker bee.   (fantasy)

A worker bee gathers sweet juice from flowers.   (fact)

Read the paragraph. <u>Underline</u> the sentences that are facts or things that can really happen.

"I'm late!" said Benny Bee. The bee flew. It went to a flower. Benny began to put the juice in a jar. His jar was not full yet. The bee flew to another flower. Soon Benny's jar was full. Benny flew back to the hive.

WRITE AWAY

Write two facts about bees.

_____

- -

_____

- -

_____

- -

_____

- -

_____

- -

101

© Houghton Mifflin Harcourt Publishing Company

Just the Right Size!

Every paragraph has a **topic.** The topic is what you are writing about. Some topics are too big. It is hard to write all the facts about the topic. Other topics are too small. There are not enough facts to tell about it.

A paragraph should tell about the topic in three or four details. That paragraph is just the right size.

Look at each pair of topics. Circle the one that would be the right size.

1. birds   how birds build nests

2. jobs horses do   horses

3. my new bike   ways to travel

4. stores   food store

WRITE AWAY

Choose one of the topics you circled.
Then get a sheet of paper.
Write three facts about the topic.

© Houghton Mifflin Harcourt Publishing Company

Writing Facts

Sometimes you will need to look in books to find facts or answer questions. An adult can help you. You should write the facts a different way. You should use different words.

A lion's roar can be heard up to five miles away.   (book fact)

A lion roars loudly.   (different words)

Read each fact. Write it a different way.

1. A community is a group of people who work and play together.

_____

- -

_____

- -

_____

2. Street signs give information that helps people move safely.

_____

- -

_____

- -

_____

WRITE AWAY

Get a sheet of paper. Then look in a book and find two facts. Ask an adult to help you. Write the facts in different words.

© Houghton Mifflin Harcourt Publishing Company

Summarizing

When you **summarize,** you tell the most important details. You tell who, what, where, when, why, and how.

Read the summary. Then answer the questions.

On Sunday, Bobby made a surprise for his dad's birthday. He made a picture. He put the picture on the table. His dad was happy when he got home.

1. Who is the paragraph about? _____

2. What is the paragraph about? _____

3. Where did Bobby put the picture? _____

4. When did he make it? _____

WRITE AWAY

Get a sheet of paper. Write a summary of a book you like. Write it in two sentences.

© Houghton Mifflin Harcourt Publishing Company

Book Titles

Sometimes you will need to look in books to find facts or answer questions. You need to write the titles.

- <u>Underline</u> the title of the book.

- Begin the first word with a capital letter.

- Important words begin with a capital letter. These words do not: <u>a</u>, <u>an</u>, <u>the</u>, <u>for</u>, <u>at</u>, and <u>in</u>.

<u>Billy and the Fire</u>

<u>The Silver Pony</u>

Look at the books. Write the titles correctly.

1.    2.

1. _____

_____

2. _____

WRITE AWAY

What is your favorite book? Write the title.

_____

_____

© Houghton Mifflin Harcourt Publishing Company

Name _____   Date _____

Parts of a Book

Books have a page with **contents.** The contents tell the parts in the book. They tell where each lesson begins.

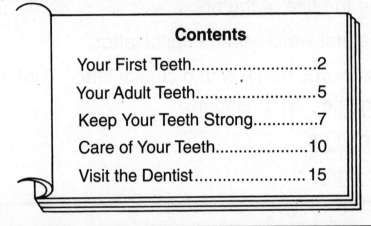

Contents

Your First Teeth.........................2

Your Adult Teeth.......................5

Keep Your Teeth Strong.............7

Care of Your Teeth....................10

Visit the Dentist.......................15

Look at the contents above. Answer the questions.

1. What page would you look at to learn about baby teeth?

_____

- -

_____

2. What page would you look at to learn about checkups?

_____

- -

_____

WRITE AWAY

Find a book that has a contents page. Ask an adult to help you. Get a sheet of paper. Write the title. Write two parts of the book. Write their page numbers.

© Houghton Mifflin Harcourt Publishing Company

Unit 7
Core Skills Writing, Grade 1

Writing: Information Paragraph

It is time to use the writing process. You will write an **information paragraph.** Just follow the steps.

Prewriting

1. What do you want to learn about? List three ideas.

   _____

   -

   _____

   -

   _____

   -

   _____

2. Are any topics too big or too small? Choose a topic that is just the right size. What will you write about?

   _____

   -

   _____

   _____

   -

   _____

   -

   _____

© Houghton Mifflin Harcourt Publishing Company

Writing: Information Paragraph, part 2

3. Look in a book. Ask an adult to help you. Write three facts about your topic. Use different words from the book.

_____

- -

_____

- -

_____

- -

_____

- -

_____

- -

_____

- -

_____

© Houghton Mifflin Harcourt Publishing Company   Core Skills Writing, Grade 1

Writing: Information Paragraph, part 3

Drafting

Write a draft of your information paragraph. Use your ideas from prewriting.

_____

- -

_____

- -

_____

- -

_____

- -

_____

- -

_____

- -

_____

- -

_____

- -

_____

- -

_____

- -

_____

- -

_____

© Houghton Mifflin Harcourt Publishing Company

Writing: Information Paragraph, part 4

Revising

Look at the sentences in your draft.

- Do you tell only facts?
- Do your facts tell only about the topic?
- Do you tell the facts in your own words?
- Do you have an ending sentence?

Share your writing with a partner. Ask your partner what needs to be changed. Ask what works well. Listen to what your partner has to say. Write your information paragraph again. Use another sheet of paper if you need to.

_____

_____

_____

_____

_____

_____

_____

_____

_____

_____

_____

© Houghton Mifflin Harcourt Publishing Company

Writing: Information Paragraph, part 5

Proofreading

Read your information paragraph three times.
Look for a different mistake each time.

Read for capital letters.

- Do all sentences begin with a capital letter?
- Do all special names begin with a capital letter?

Read for end marks and commas.

- Is a comma used when three or more things are listed?
- Do all sentences have an end mark?

Read for spelling and spaces.

- Is the first word indented in the paragraph?
- Are all words spelled correctly?

≡	Use a capital letter.
/	Use a lowercase letter.
⊙	Add a period.
∧	Add something.
✗	Take out something.
∧	Change something.
○	Check the spelling.

Use the Proofreading Marks to fix the mistakes on page 110.

Publishing

Now you are ready to share your information paragraph. Use a computer or page 112 to publish your work.

- Write a title.
- Write in your best handwriting. You can also use the tips on page 11 to publish on a computer.
- Draw a picture to go along with your paragraph.
- Get a large sheet of construction paper. Paste your paragraph and picture on it.

© Houghton Mifflin Harcourt Publishing Company

Name _____ Date _____

_____

Title _____

_____

_____

_____

_____

_____

_____

_____

_____

_____

_____

_____

_____

_____

_____

_____

© Houghton Mifflin Harcourt Publishing Company

Opinion Paragraph

An **opinion paragraph** tells how you believe or feel about something. The first sentence in the paragraph is your opinion sentence. An opinion sentence shows strong feeling. Sometimes an opinion sentence ends with an exclamation mark. The second part of an opinion paragraph includes reasons. List your reasons. Put the most important reason last.

> Rex and Jim is the funniest book ever! (opinion sentence)
>
> Rex is a dog, but he wants to be a cat. (reason)
>
> He always eats cat food. (reason)
>
> He made whiskers and put them on his face. (reason)

These sentences are from an opinion paragraph. They are not in the correct order. Write O for opinion or R for reason.

1. It has bars to climb on.

   _____

   - - - - - - - - - - - - - - - -

   _____

2. Our school playground is great!

   _____

   - - - - - - - - - - - - - - - -

   _____

3. The basketball court is big.

   _____

   - - - - - - - - - - - - - - - -

   _____

4. It has a new slide.

   _____

   - - - - - - - - - - - - - - - -

   _____

WRITE AWAY

Get a sheet of paper. How do you feel about your school playground? Write your opinion. Make a list of reasons.

© Houghton Mifflin Harcourt Publishing Company

Opinion Paragraph, part 2

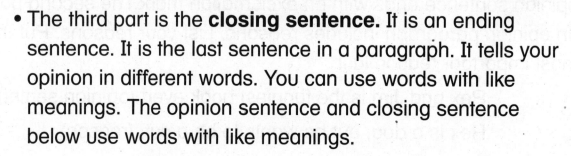

An **opinion paragraph** has several parts.

- The first part gives an opinion in a topic sentence.

- The second part includes reasons.

- The third part is the **closing sentence.** It is an ending sentence. It is the last sentence in a paragraph. It tells your opinion in different words. You can use words with like meanings. The opinion sentence and closing sentence below use words with like meanings.

   We saw the <u>funniest</u> clown at the circus! He made faces and blew a horn. He did tricks with his pet pig. He was the <u>silliest</u> clown I've ever seen.

Read each opinion sentence. Then use different words to write a closing sentence.

1. Mario is the nicest boy in first grade.

   _____

   _____

2. The new roller coaster is the most thrilling ride ever!

   _____

   _____

WRITE AWAY

What kind of food do you think is best? Why? Get a sheet of paper. Write an opinion paragraph. Use different words in your closing sentence.

© Houghton Mifflin Harcourt Publishing Company

Name _____ Date _____

Words That Compare

Describing words can tell how things are different from each other. Add er to words that compare two things. Add est to compare more than two things.

long   long**er**   long**est**

Look at each picture. Add **er** or **est** to the describing words to tell about the pictures in each row. Use **tall** and **small**.

1.

_____   _____   _____
- - - - - - - - - - - - - - - - - - -   - - - - - - - - - - - - - - - - - - -   - - - - - - - - - - - - - - - - - - -
_____   _____   _____

2.

_____   _____   _____
- - - - - - - - - - - - - - - - - - -   - - - - - - - - - - - - - - - - - - -   - - - - - - - - - - - - - - - - - - -
_____   _____   _____

WRITE AWAY

Work with two other friends. Look at your pencils. Then get a sheet of paper. Write sentences that compare the pencils.

© Houghton Mifflin Harcourt Publishing Company

Writing a Book Report

A **book report** tells what a book is about. A book report has several parts.

- A book report gives an opinion about the book. The opinion sentence tells readers how the writer feels about the book.

- A book report tells the title of the book and the author's name.

- A book report tells the main idea of the book without telling the ending. It gives reasons that tell why the writer liked the book.

- A book report has a closing sentence. It tells an opinion in different words.

Read Kate's book report. Then follow the directions below.

Everyone should read the funny book A Purple Pizza by Star Ving! First, a boy named Ned cooks a purple pizza! Next, he asks the lunch workers at school to sell it. Then Ned eats a slice, and his lips turn purple! He doesn't know what to do. I think everyone will enjoy this very funny book.

1. Circle the title of the book in red.

2. Circle Kate's opinion of the book in blue.

3. Circle the name of the author in green.

4. Write one reason Kate likes the book.

_____

- -

_____

5. Circle the closing sentence in yellow.

Writing: Opinion Paragraph

It is time to use the writing process. You will write an opinion paragraph about a favorite book. Just follow these steps.

Prewriting

1. What are some of your favorite books? List two books. Then choose one book to write about.

_____

_____

_____

2. What is your opinion of this book?

_____

_____

_____

3. What are some reasons for your opinion?

_____

_____

_____

© Houghton Mifflin Harcourt Publishing Company

Writing: Opinion Paragraph, part 2

Drafting

Write a draft of your opinion paragraph about a favorite book. Use your ideas from prewriting.

_____

- -

_____

- -

_____

- -

_____

- -

_____

- -

_____

- -

_____

- -

_____

- -

_____

- -

_____

- -

_____

- -

_____

© Houghton Mifflin Harcourt Publishing Company

Writing: Opinion Paragraph, part 3

Revising

Look at the sentences in your draft.

- Do you give your opinion in a topic sentence?

- Do your reasons tell about your opinion?

- Do you use exact words to make the ideas clear?

- Do you have a closing sentence?

Share your writing with a partner. Listen to his or her comments. Write your opinion paragraph again. Use another sheet of paper if you need to.

_____

- -

_____

- -

_____

- -

_____

- -

_____

- -

_____

- -

_____

© Houghton Mifflin Harcourt Publishing Company

Writing: Opinion Paragraph, part 4

Proofreading

Read your opinion paragraph three times. Look for a different mistake each time.

☰	Use a capital letter.
/	Use a lowercase letter.
⊙	Add a period.
∧	Add something.
⤙	Take out something.
⋏	Change something.
◯	Check the spelling.

Read for capital letters.

- Do all sentences begin with a capital letter?
- Do all special names begin with a capital letter?

Read for end marks and commas.

- Is there a comma when three or more things are listed?
- Do all sentences have an end mark?

Read for spelling and spaces.

- Is the first word in the paragraph indented?
- Are all words spelled correctly?

Use the Proofreading Marks to fix the mistakes on page 119.

Publishing

Now you are ready to share your opinion paragraph. Use a computer or page 121 to publish your work.

- Write a title.
- Write in your best handwriting. You can also use the tips on page 11 to publish on a computer.
- Draw a picture to go along with your paragraph.
- Get a large sheet of construction paper. Paste your paragraph and picture on it.

© Houghton Mifflin Harcourt Publishing Company

Name _____ Date _____

Title _____

© Houghton Mifflin Harcourt Publishing Company

Name _____ Date _____

Journal Paper

_____
- -

Date _____

Dear Journal,

_____
- -
_____
- -
_____
- -
_____
- -
_____

© Houghton Mifflin Harcourt Publishing Company

The Writing Process

There are five steps in the writing process.

Prewriting

Choose an idea. Then plan what you will write.
Use lists, webs, and pictures to help you.

Drafting

Write words and sentences. You will fix the
mistakes later.

Revising

Change words and sentences in your writing.
Make the writing better.

Proofreading

Read your writing to look for mistakes in capital letters,
end marks, and spelling.

Publishing

Make a clean copy of your writing on paper or on the
computer. Then share your work!

© Houghton Mifflin Harcourt Publishing Company

Name _____   Date _____

Proofreading Checklist

Read your writing three times. Look for a different mistake each time.

Read for capital letters.

☐ Do all sentences begin with a capital letter?

☐ Do all special names begin with a capital letter?

☐ Do the names of months and dates begin with a capital letter?

☐ Does the word I have a capital letter?

Read for end marks and commas.

☐ Is a comma used when three or more things are listed?

☐ Do all sentences have an end mark?

Read for spelling and spaces.

☐ Is the first word in the paragraph indented?

☐ Are all words spelled correctly?

© Houghton Mifflin Harcourt Publishing Company

Proofreading Marks

Use these special marks to show the mistakes in your writing.

≡	Use a capital letter.
/	Use a lowercase letter.
⊙	Add a period.
∧	Add something.
ٯ	Take out something.
⌒	Change something.
○	Check the spelling.

© Houghton Mifflin Harcourt Publishing Company

Name _____ Date _____

Language Tips

Using Capital Letters

Use capital letters for

• the beginning of a sentence.	**We** play.
• the names of people.	My name is **P**at.
• the names of pets.	My cat is **W**inky.
• the name of each day.	Today is **M**onday.
• the name of each month.	Is it cold in **M**arch?
• the names of places.	I live on **S**ixth **S**treet.

Adding Endings to Words

Add s to many naming words to make them mean more than one.	one bug three bugs
Add s to most action words to tell what one person or thing does today.	He walks. She jumps.
Add ed to most action words to tell what happened in the past.	He walked. She jumped.

Using Periods, Question Marks, and Commas

End telling sentences with a **period.**	I skated**.**
End asking sentences with a **question mark.**	What is your name**?**
Use a **comma** between the day and year in a date.	November 24**,** 2013

Using A and An

Use an before words that begin with a vowel (a, e, i, o, and u).	an apple an owl
Use a before words that begin with a consonant.	a boat a car

126

Answer Key

Student answers will vary on the pages not included in this Answer Key. Accept all reasonable answers.

Page 3
1. letter
2. poster
3. story

Page 4
1. C
2. B
3. A

Page 9
It was my birthday⑦ We went to the ㉿zo⦁ ⓤ was fun.

Page 10
My ⟨frend⟩ ţed called me⦁ He asked me to go to the Ꝑark. I said yes. It would be fun to go
to
∧ the park.

Page 13
1. no
2. yes
3. no
4. yes

Page 16
1. The cat hissed.
2. The cat ran up the tree.
3. The dog barked at the cat.

Page 21
1. She saw a crab. It bit her toe.
2. Kim yelled. She ran away.

Page 22
1. The dog is dirty.
2. The girl gets a tub.
3. She gives the dog a bath.

Page 23
1. Jack and jill went up a Ⱨill.
2. Little miss Muffet sat on a tuffet⦁
3. Do ⓤ know the ~~the~~ muffin man?

Page 30
1. thing
2. place
3. person

Page 32
1. balls
2. kites
3. bears
4. cars

Page 33
1. dishes
2. boxes
3. dresses
4. wrenches

Page 35
Children cross out the picture of Cat holding a gift.

Page 36
1. Children circle *Lita and I played a game.*
2. Children circle *I swam with my friend today.*
3. Children circle *I played soccer with my friends.*

Page 38
Order: 3, 1, 2

Page 47
1. sleep
2. eat
3. read

Page 50
1. swims
2. swam
3. took
4. takes

Page 53
Children write a comma in the following places:
October 25, 2014
Dear Lisa,
Sincerely,

Page 56
1. She watered the flowers.
2. They are tall.
3. He picks a flower.

Page 62
Possible answers:
It was brown.
It had long ears.
It had a white fluffy tail.
The rabbit was eating carrots.

Page 67
Most likely answers:
1. mad
2. scared
3. happy
4. tired
5. sad
6. surprised

Page 68
1. John sat down and rested.
2. John ate an apple and honey.
3. He saw a bee and a kitten.

Page 69
1. Jed and Ed came to the party.
2. Jan and Ann got presents.
3. The girls and boys played games.

Page 70
1. Eva called Jen, Jo, and Tom.
2. Rabbit, Bear, and Kitten will go.

© Houghton Mifflin Harcourt Publishing Company

Answer Key
Core Skills Writing, Grade 1

Page 71

Answers will vary. Possible answer:
Fox was hungry and looked for food.
Fox saw some grapes. The grapes were
too high. Fox was not happy and left.

Page 73

1. Children underline *John's feet* and
   stinky garbage. Both smell bad.
2. Children underline *children* and
   rabbits. Both ran quickly.

Page 85

1. First
2. Then/Next
3. Finally/Soon

Page 87

1. tall
2. angry
3. raced

Page 88

1. cold
2. dry
3. close
4. dirty

Page 89

1. to
2. buy
3. sees
4. four

Page 91

1. There is an easy way to blow up
   a balloon.
2. Blowing up a balloon is easy.

Page 92

1. b
2. d
3. c
4. a

Page 93

Possible answers:
1. Add a step saying that the seeker
   closes his or her eyes.
2. Add a step saying that the seeker
   counts to ten.

Page 100

1. Frogs have long legs.
2. Possible answers from which
   children choose one:
   It can jump on land.
   It can swim in water.
   It will hop away from
   animals that will eat it.
   It will swim away from animals
   that will eat it.

Page 101

Children underline these sentences:
The bee flew.
It went to a flower.
The bee flew to another flower.

Page 102

1. how birds build nests
2. jobs horses do
3. my new bike
4. food store

Page 104

1. Bobby
2. making a picture/making a surprise
3. on the table
4. Sunday

Page 105

1. Max and Jen
2. The Big Fish

Page 106

1. 2
2. 15

Page 113

1. R
2. O
3. R
4. R

Page 115

1. tallest, taller, tall
2. smaller, small, smallest

Page 116

1. Children circle *A Purple Pizza*
   in red.
2. Children circle *Everyone should
   read the funny book A Purple
   Pizza by Star Ving!* in blue.
3. Children circle *Star Ving* in green.
4. Answers will vary.
5. Children circle *I think everyone
   will enjoy this very funny book.*
   in yellow.

© Houghton Mifflin Harcourt Publishing Company